Canary Park © 2025 by Damiek Barrow

All rights reserved, including the right to reproduction of this book in whole or in any part in any form.

ISBN 978-1-7364332-4-9

Damiekbarrow7@gmail.com

Zigzagzig.net

@damiekbarrow

Illustrated by: Amirah Barrow

Amirahbarrow03@gmail.com

@printshop.princess

Canary Park was first written and produced by:

- Students at Washington Preparatory High School, 2016
- Loyola Marymount University by Upward Bound Students, 2018
- Susan Miller Dorsey High School students casted, produced and directed by Mrs. Horton, 2023

Canary Park

Meet the playwright

Damiek Barrow is an educator who lives in Inglewood, CA. He graduated from California State University Northridge, with a Bachelor's Degree in English/Creative Writing and holds Master's degrees in Education and Administration. Damiek embraces a simple life of family, exercise, travel, learning and teaching. He encourages students and fellow educators to learn their culture, find their voice and use it to better themselves and their communities.

His works include the novel "***Zig Zag Zig***."

"***Popcorn and Hot Sauce***" a collection of poetry and essays.

Stage plays: "***Jumping the Broom***"

"***The 12 Jewels***" and "***Randy's Party***."

Canary Park

Gratitude and love to the family and friends who shared unconditional support.

- Barbados and all of the Caribbean
- Southeast London, United Kingdom
- Miami-Dade County, Florida
- Far Rockaway, Queens and Roosevelt, New York
- Toronto and Winnipeg, Canada
- Simi Valley, CA
- Tuscaloosa, Alabama
- Inglewood, CA

Canary Park

This project is dedicated to the babies.
We are a resilient people who
Rise and overcome all conditions,
All the time.
The world is yours.

Canary Park

Canary

Usually interpreted as a happy symbol, an uncaged canary represents freedom, and intellectual self expression. If depicted in a cage, it represents entrapment and sometimes unhappiness.

Its past use was as a measure for air quality in the mines. If scent less poisonous gasses were present, the bird would immediately die, which in turn saved the minor's lives. Today, a canary is still connected to self-sacrifice and innocence.

Canary Park

The scene is set in modern day Los Angeles in an urban community park with a bench, street light and a trash can.

The snitch rule is a conflict within itself. In our communities, there is an unwritten rule that it is taboo to cooperate with law enforcement, who historically has not supported us as a whole. Citizens who witness or experience crimes often keep it to themselves. Those who speak up, are often ostracized or harmed. Perhaps the intention is to discipline the perpetrators ourselves, but what does that honestly look like and how often does it occur? This conflict often leaves the community at the mercy of predators who take advantage of the silent code.

Canary Park

Essential questions

1. If you witness a crime that brings harm to members of a family or community, will you stay silent or speak up?
2. How do we police our own community if we do not want the law involved with our affairs?
3. Whose responsibility is it to protect the innocent?

Canary Park

Characters

RayRay- *Burdened*

YG- *Capitalist*

Ced- *Beloved*

Pops- *Devoted*

Fatimah- *Virtuous*

Junebug- *Shaman-A prop and character.*

Twins- *Obsessed*

Chorus- *Oracles- Their characters are represented by the symbols:*

  +   and   --

Canary Park

Table of Contents

Act 1
Scene 1- page 9
Scene 2- page 16
Scene 3-page 23
Scene 4- page 34
Scene 5- page 48

Act 2
Scene 1- page 73
Scene 2-page 104
Scene 3-page 117
Scene 4-page 122
Scene 5-page 138

Canary Park

ACT I Scene 1

(Enter Junebug, who resembles a homeless man dressed in rags pushing a shopping cart filled with his belongings. He finds treasures that others fail to see. His slow and methodical movement blends in with his environment effortlessly.)

Chorus <u>Two males</u>

+

You heard YG is trying to get put on?

--

YG? He'll be even more careless if he gets put on. Think he will make a positive impact, you're dead wrong.

Remember the twins who used to live around the way?

+

Yeah, yeah. I saw them the other day.

--

YG stole their momma's jewelry box.

Canary Park

They are searching and seeking.

If they find YG, they will delete him.

+

He gotta see RayRay first.

RayRay is Papa, the real Papa Smurf.

--

RayRay ain't messing with YG. He's bad luck. Betcha Rock, paper, scissors, YG gonna do what he does consistently....Blow things up.

+

I asked RayRay if he needed my services and he told me the streets weren't ready for me. I'm too much of a "G."

--

Stop lying Bro you ain't no gangster.

You'd live longer being a backup dancer.

+

But I do have some gangster tendencies.

Like, the way I beat you in basketball.

Canary Park

That whipping is still trauma in your memory.

\--

You ain't beat me since I was 8 and I had a broken arm.

\+

A win is a win. I got skills like I was raised on a basketball farm.

\--

You still owe me money from the last game.

You don't pay up, I put you to shame.

\+

I don't remember.

\--

Stop lying.

\+

I'm not lying. I put that on my Mama.

\--

Whatever Bro you ain't nothing but drama.

Canary Park

(They exit. RayRay enters, looking around, waiting. RayRay has a solid, commanding presence that makes him appear larger than he actually is. His deep voice and slow speaking cadence intimidates many, but his greatest weapon is his intelligence.

YG arrives on the scene. Slight in build, his eyes are always scanning, head is continuously on a swivel like a scavenger searching for opportunities or danger. He carries a black backpack filled with contempt.)

RayRay

Did you handle that?

YG

It's going down tonight. Don't worry about it. I got you.

RayRay

You said that yesterday. You costing me money.

YG

We didn't have a driver.

RayRay

Canary Park

I thought Tank was supposed to drive.

YG

Tank has car problems.

RayRay

Who's driving tonight?

YG

Ced.

RayRay

Ced? How you pull that off?

YG

He thinks I just need a ride.

RayRay

What does that mean?

YG

He don't need to know the business. I just need him to give me a ride. That's my bro. He always looks out for me.

RayRay

That's not how we get down. You leaving us open with an outsider.

YG

Everybody knows Ced. He's the golden boy of the hood.

RayRay

So what...This isn't his style.

YG

But...

RayRay

But nothing...You ain't listening fool. Find another driver and leave Ced alone. I don't want him involved. Period. You're already two days behind. Step your game up or I'm a take care of it....Then take care of you.

YG

Hey RayRay with all due respect, I don't like the way you be talking to me.

RayRay

Canary Park

Do something about it then. Complete the task. Earn your respect. **(Walks up to YG's space forcing him to back up and submit. Satisfied, RayRay turns around and walks off. YG walks behind RayRay mocking him until RayRay turns around, YG puts his head down.)**

Act 1 Scene 2

(Pops enters with his bag containing his chess pieces and a portable table. He unpacks his tools and sits at the bench focused on his game board. Pops is a disciplined and stoic man who is immaculately dressed. He looks around the park and waves at Ced.

Ced is his grandson. Ced also carries a black backpack filled with responsibility. He's an overachiever who embraces challenges. He walks with purpose and focus. His ambition often makes him forget to enjoy the simple pleasures of life.)

Pops

Ced!

Ced

What up Pops!

Pops

Don't what up me, boy.

Save that slang for someone your age.

Canary Park

Ced

Yes Sir.

Pops

You finished your chores?

Ced

Yes Sir.

Pops

Homework?

Ced

I'm ahead of all my projects, Pops.

Pops

Did you call about that job? I put a word in for you. Don't make me look bad.

Ced

Yes, Pops. I got it. I got the job.

Pops

You got it? **(changes his body language to a happy tone.)**

Canary Park

Well now, that's a big deal. You're on your way, Son. It's all about time management now. You didn't need another job, but I love your work ethic.

Ced

My orientation is tomorrow. **(shaking hands)** I told you Pops.

Pops

What's the rush?

Ced

My goal is to get our own space by graduation.

Pops

I respect that. Trust me. You need to consider not signing a lease until after you complete bootcamp. You might get stationed in another county or state. Be patient. Save your money. Send for Fatimah and CJ after you learn your assignment. The Air Force takes care of their people.

Ced

Canary Park

That makes sense Pops. I'll still stack my money. Wanted to ask you something.

Pops

Is everything okay?

Ced

I'm good. After I graduate, what are you going to do? If I do get stationed outside of LA, you'll be alone.

Pops

Haven't thought about it. Been so focused on getting you to the finish line.

Ced

That's a done deal Pops. I'll walk across that stage in a few months.

Pops

Get out of the city maybe. Who knows? I have options.

(makes a few thoughtful moves on the chessboard.

Ced studies the board, then makes a move.)

That was a good move, Son. Yes. Always protect your Queen.

Ced

You think you'll remarry? It's been 4 years since..... Grandma died. Pops. Maybe it's time for you to find someone to enjoy life with. I don't want you to be by yourself if we leave.

Pops

Your grandmother was my soulmate and everything I ever wanted in a woman. I doubt I can ever love like that again, furthermore marry, but I can have a little fun now and then. Know what I mean? **(playful laughter)**

Ced

What?!! This is news to me. Pops, you be outside?

Pops

Son....You have to be outside in order to get inside. You're not the only one who goes out at night. You be sneaking. I be creeping. **(they both laugh, leaning on each other, comfortably**

Canary Park

familiar.) So, what time are you going to be home?

Ced

I won't be too late Pops, about to meet Fatimah in a few minutes.

Pops

Tell her to come by and bring CJ, my lil king. I haven't seen them all week.

Ced

Yes sir.

Pops

Well, I played three games of chess today. About to go home to cook supper, listen to some Aretha and relax.

Ced

How can you play chess and dominoes every day?

Pops

Part of my routine. Go to the gym, do some volunteer work, play a few games here. They're games of strategy and patience and good for the brain.

Ced

Whatever makes you happy Pop, keep doing it. I'll see you later.

Pop

(grabs his bag and begins to walk off before turning around) Love you son. I'm very proud of you. I wish your mom and Grandma could be here to see the man you've turned into.

Ced

Thanks Pop...Love you too....

Act 1 Scene 3

(Enter Fatimah, a beautiful young lady. Her aura is captivating and bold. Her confident energy is contagious. She sneaks up playfully behind Ced and covers her hands over his eyes.)

Fatimah

Guess who?

Ced

Hmm. Can I get a hint?

Fatimah

It's the love of your life.

Ced

I need more info.

Fatimah

(acting shocked but playing along with him.) Your high school sweetheart…

Ced

Ah… Still can't guess…Give me a hint.

Fatimah

The mother of your son.

Ced

Oh Grace....

Fatimah

(balls up her fist with genuine attitude) Grace? Who is Grace?

Ced

(laughing while holding her hands) I'm only playing. I knew it was you, Fatimah.

Fatimah

You already know. Grace and you were gonna come up missing. Keep playing with me and find out.

Ced

Come on, you know you the only girl for me. **(they hug and Fatimah sits down beside him.)** How's my Boo? You had a good day?

Fatimah

I'm great. My day was chill. **(laying in his arms)** It just got a whole lot better though. I missed you.

Ced

I missed you too. How's my baby boy doing?

Fatimah

Bad...Crying if no one picks him up. Putting everything in his mouth. He's with my Mom at choir practice.

Ced

Pops wants to spend some time. He just asked about ya'll.

Fatimah

I know. I miss Pops too. It's been a minute.

So when are we going to spend some time together?

Ced

We're together now...Tima.

Fatimah

You know what I mean. Between work, school and CJ, we lose track. Let's go to a movie.

Ced

Not tonight. I have to get up early. I got that other part time job. Orientation is until 1:00 tomorrow.

(enter YG, who sneaks in behind them undetected.)

Fatimah

Two jobs Ced? How are you going to manage school and….us?

Ced

It'll take a little while to get used to. By graduation, we'll have enough money saved for our own place. Actually, Pops was telling me to wait until I know where I'll be stationed.

Fatimah

We talked about that, remember? Be still Baby. You don't have to do everything at one time, by yourself. We're supposed to do this together.

Ced

See, **(hugs her)** that's what I love about you.

Fatimah

You already know.

So tell Pops I'll stop by tomorrow. I'll be there when you get home.

Ced

Pops will love that. We'll spend the day together after I handle my chores. Promise.

Fatimah

Yaay!! Love you Baby.

Ced

Love you too…. Grace.

Fatimah

(Stands up, changes her mood to serious with hand on hip, neck and finger focused on Ced) You know what…Boy…..Don't get yourself cut. Be bleeding the first day on your new job.

Ced

(laughing) I love that thug in you. You act all sophisticated, then explode from zero to a hundred. Come on. I'll walk you to your car.

Fatimah

I'm serious about mine. You already know.

(they begin walking when YG makes his presence known.)

YG

(exaggerated movement) Hey yo! Ced! I need to holla at you! Ced!

Ced

(Fatimah instantly is agitated and tries to drag Ced on, but he acknowledges YG.) Hold up YG. I need to walk Fatimah to her car.

YG

(stares at Fatimah while rubbing his hands in a lustful way) Can't say hi Fatimah?

Fatimah

Canary Park

(Fatimah looks him up and down disapprovingly, shakes her head and sucks her teeth.)

Hi.

(turns her back to YG and faces Ced) It's okay Baby. I'll see you later. Can you pick up some diapers for CJ, please? He's almost out.

Ced

Okay. I'll bring them in a few. **(Fatima hugs Ced and exits as both men watch her.)**

YG

Bye Fatimah…..Must be nice…..Ced.

Ced

You staring too hard bro, and what're you talking about?

YG

You know… **(walking around imitating Ced with exaggerated importance)** Mr. All American athlete who turned down scholarships to serve his country, honor roll, Mr. Homecoming King, got the finest girl around the way. She even gave you a baby boy. You living the American dream.

Ced

Sounds like you are writing a book about my life.

YG

It must be nice...that's all. The rest of us trying hard to make it on these streets.

Ced

Here we go.

YG

Nah...I ain't hating. Fatimah chose you. She didn't want me. I'm over it. Here's some advice **(looks around and whispers in his ear)** You can't trust women Ced. Remember that.

Ced

Here's my advice to you, mind your business and stop staring so much.

YG

It's not to be disrespectful Ced. She catches everyone's eye. Sometimes, I think about what could have been if we were still together. That's it. I know that's your woman. The whole world knows.

Ced

First of all, you never had her. I'm nothing special YG. I came up in the same place, at the same time, in these same streets watching all that comes with it just like you. I play sports. I don't play the streets. **(checking the time, growing impatient)** So what you need? I have work to do.

YG

You are always working on something Ced. Listen. I need a ride to the Eastside. I have to ask about a job. Drop me off back here at the park. It's on the way.

Ced

(thinking) Man. It's Friday night, been a long week. I'm not trying to get caught up with your bs.

YG

Come on… That's how you do your boy? I got you Ced. I'll give you $20 for your gas and time.

Ced

(thinking, fighting his thoughts.) Alright YG.

(YG attempts to shake his hand but Ced slaps it away.) Where's the money?

YG

And that's why you're my best friend.**(YG hands him $20. Ced holds it up to the light to see if it's real.) (fantasizing)** Can we get some nachos like old times? Dripping with melted cheese, steak, jalapenos and **(he dramatically word plays and dances with a Latino accent.)** pico de ga-llo, de ga-llo, ga-llo and green sauce.

Ced

No…we ain't making stops. I have to pick up some diapers, give my son a bath and put him to sleep.

YG

Man you ain't no fun. You'd rather hang out with Fatimah and CJ instead of me?

Canary Park

Ced

Every single second, hour, minute and day of the week. Come on. Let's go.

YG

Bro.... You are a whole grown man. **(mockingly)** I have to give CJ a bath, put him to sleep, file my taxes and fix the water heater.

Ced

(laughing) Shut your big head up.

(they exit)

Canary Park

Act 1 Scene 4

(later that afternoon)

Chorus

Two teenage girls

+

What happened?

--

I'm so mad at her right now. She told Mama that I was smoking and missing class. My mama went off and that makes me go off.

+

She told?

--

Yes girl, my own sister. It's bad enough you got snitches on the streets but to have one in your own family is crazy. When I see her I'm going to go off.

+

Canary Park

Well that's not really snitching, she was looking out for you. These kids are lacing stuff with fentanyl and other drugs just to see what happens to you. I been told you that.

--

You sound just like my sister. She still didn't have any business ratting me out. Don't get me started. I will go off.

+

Girl. That's because you don't listen to anybody. And snitching is complicated.

--

It's not complicated. Just keep your mouth shut. Girl. Do you want me to go off?

+

I mean, when you think about it, people are just telling the truth. Sis was trying to protect you when you didn't listen. You started to slip.

--

Canary Park

I don't care. Anytime you tell someone else's business then you're a snitch. If they don't know, I'll go off and make sure they know.

+

But it's different. That's your family. My brother said it's snitching when you do a crime with someone, get caught, then tell on everybody who was involved. Or if you're in a grocery store and see someone stealing food. We mind our own business. It doesn't have anything to do with us. That person is probably starving.

--

Girl. Who's side are you on anyway?

+

Nobody's side. I'm just saying. Ever notice how our generation protects predators, not the innocent?

--

Oh you about to make me go off.

+

You always going off on someone.

Canary Park

\--

You know why? Because everybody in my house is a snitch, except me. I can't go out for the rest of the month, Mama took my phone and will be drug testing me once a week. Now I have to go home and hear her mouth. Mama is a snitch too. She told everybody in the family.

+

Don't you hate that? They all have something to say. It all starts with "when I was a kid." Nobody is trying to hear what you did in the late 1900s, Uncle Mike.

\--

Girl I'm lectured out. They take turns telling me the same thing. When I get off punishment, I'm a go off. Anyway, let me get home before my mama starts acting up and goes off. Then I go off, then she knocks my head off.

+

Alright girl. I'll see you in the morning.

Canary Park

(RayRay enters. He is communicating and gesturing while on the phone, sending texts and moving with business-like urgency. Finally he sits waiting at a bench, checking the time. YG is obviously proud of himself for some reason demonstrated by his runway model walk with a backpack in hand.)

YG

Hi. (waves at him)

RayRay

You're late. And don't be waving at me. Brothers don't say hi and wave to each other. Weirdo.

YG

What up with you Big Homie Gangster Lokeness. **(extends his hand but RayRay ignores him.)** RayRay, you gonna leave me hanging?

RayRay

Shut up...You got something for me?

YG

Canary Park

(hands him a backpack) Here you go. I told you I'd come through. You doubted me. I saw it in your eyes.

RayRay

(opens the backpack, inspects the content and throws the bag at YG's chest)

Pampers and baby formula? What is this a joke?

YG

What the? **(looks inside the package and immediately has a childish tantrum before he regains control himself.)**

There must be a mistake…**(thinking out loud while pacing.)** I must have took the wrong backpack and left mine in Ced's car.

RayRay

What the hell is it doing in Ced's car? I told you to leave him out of it. **(takes a deep breath to calm himself)** Now, where is my work?

YG

Did I say Ced?...No my bad... Not Ced..... I meant to say Ed..... my homey Ed from way back. I'll call him and we can fix this real quick. Hold on.

(RayRay looks around, lifts up his shirt and reaches for his weapon as YG panics and puts his hands up) Come on RayRay. I can make this right man. You don't have to do this.

(RayRay hears someone approaching and puts back down his shirt to conceal the weapon.)

RayRay

Shut up.

(Enter Fatimah, she is aggressive in her movement, and upset. RayRay moves away from them, listening from a distance.)

Fatimah

YG! **(she pushes YG)** What did you do?

YG

What're you talking about?

Fatimah

Canary Park

Don't act like you don't know what I'm talking about. Cops pulled Ced over and found a backpack full of money, guns, meth and God knows what else. They arrested him right in front of me and CJ.

YG

Whaaat? Noooo....Not Ced. **(He gestures trying desperately to quiet Fatimah, hoping that RayRay did not hear the news.)** Why would you think that I'm involved?

Fatimah

YG.... You were with him last. I know that was your bag. Ced doesn't move like that.

YG

Fatimah, I don't even know what you're talking about. I asked him to take me to my Aunt's house to pick up some chicken enchiladas. I don't know nothing about guns, meth or money. I came back here and have been chopping it up with RayRay this whole time. Ask him. **(RayRay looks at Fatimah, then at YG and shakes his head in disgust. He walks off stage.)**

Canary Park

Fatimah

I can't believe this is happening to us.

(Fatimah sits, puts her head in her hands and rocks back and forth. YG attempts to comfort her with a hug, she jumps up and pushes him away.)

Get off me. Don't ever put your hands on me.

YG

Come on. Don't be like that Tima. I was just trying to calm you down.

Fatimah

My name is Fatimah. You **(pointing her finger in his face)** You don't... get... to call me Tima! You haven't earned that. First you got my Ced caught up, now you're trying to put your filthy hands on me.

YG

Feisty lady. **(makes a growling sound.)** I like that. Well it happens. You didn't know everything about your man, huh? Ced led a double life. He was trying to make some extra cash to take care of you and...

Fatimah

Liar!

YG

You're not even trying to hear me. **(stares at her, then attempts to sit on the bench, Fatimah immediately rises to separate herself from him.)**

What you see in him anyway?

Fatimah

Unlike you YG.

He's responsible and hard working.

No one respects you.

Everywhere you go, you cause problems.

You make me sick.

YG

Well damn Tima. Be honest. Tell me how you really feel.

Canary Park

Fatimah

It's Fatimah! Fa- ti- mah! And you on my last nerve.

YG

That's cold Fatimah. I'm hurt by your words.

Fatimah

You need to be human for your feelings to be hurt. You're beneath that.

YG

Ouch! You throwing daggers to my heart.**(acting as though his heart has been pierced)**

Fatimah

So you're just going to let Ced take the blame? **(walks up to YG with hands on her hips)**

You need to go down to the police station and tell them what you did. Right now.

YG

(looking around, moving closer, laughing at her.) Yea right, that will never happen. You must be crazy. Look. Fatimah. I'm kind of busy right now.

Fatimah

You're pathetic. **(Fatimah turns arounds)** I hate you.

YG

You don't mean that. You're an emotional wreck right now, but you're going to need me soon. Remember my words. I'll be there for you in ways that Ced could never do. Matter of fact, I picked up some pampers for CJ.

Fatimah

(YG offers her the backpack....Fatimah unzips it and looks at the contents in disbelief. She closes the bag.)

This is Ced's bag.... Where's his wallet and phone? **(YG shrugs his shoulders as if he does not know.)**

Why are you like this? **(she throws the bag in the trashcan and exits.)**

YG

Canary Park

(YG takes the bag out of the trash, dusts it off and puts it on his shoulders.)

You're gonna need me Fatimah.

Call me **323 333 4444** that's **323 333 4444!**

Once again **323 333 4444!!!**

Don't be scared of this gangster love.

(looks around, laughs nervously and takes out his phone and makes a call.)

Grandma, how are you?

It's Yafe.

I'm fine Grandma.

I miss you too.

Was thinking about visiting.

No, I'm not in trouble.

I'll catch a Greyhound and be there by tomorrow morning.

Yes, everything is fine.

Promise.

Canary Park

I just want to see you.

Okay I'll see you later.

Love you too.

(hangs up. From nervous to calm confidence he looks directly at the audience.)

All of you expect the worst from me. Don't you?

Ok.

Bet.

I'll give you exactly what you looking for.

Watch.

(He runs off stage. Moments later, two people run on stage with an urgency. They are dressed the same and their movements mirror each other. Clearly, they are frustrated as if they are too late and missed an opportunity. It's the twins, looking for YG.)

Canary Park

Act 1 Scene 5

(Colors on stage represent days and nights as time passes and life goes on.

Junebug enters,

looks up at the sky and spreads

his arms to feel the sun or moon.

He looks around the stage,

takes out a rag and wipes down the bench,

takes a book from his cart ,

sits and begins reading.)

<u>Chorus</u>

<u>Two males</u>

+

Ced caught a case. He's looking at 15-20 years in solitary confinement.

--

You lying!

Canary Park

+

Cops caught him in a giant Uhaul truck filled with about 1000 assault weapons, about $500gs in cash, two keys, 100 pounds of meth and a cage full of exotic monkeys.

--

(laughs) Monkeys bro...You always put extras on everything ...Who told you? Matter of fact, I know you lying.

+

What? I was there when Ced told me the plan. Bro, he asked me to drive for him. I was about to, but Alexis came over and well, you know. I had to handle my business.

--

Stop lying Bro. Ced didn't get arrested for anything like that. And, I know for sure that you didn't hook up with Alexis. You ain't had sex since sex had you.

+

Canary Park

You don't know what I do. Was you there? No. You never believe me.

--

That's because you always be lying. For why?

+

I put that on everything.

--

Just because you put your word on something doesn't mean you telling the truth. I heard you put stuff on the hood, dead homies, and relatives 100 times before and you were still lying. For why?

+

When did I ever lie to you about?

--

You lied when you said your family were millionaires.

You lied about being on the honor roll.

You lied about Jada being your girlfriend.

Canary Park

You lied about going to jail.

You're probably lying right now about Ced, especially about monkeys and Alexis.

+

I did go to jail.

--

Yea, to visit a relative.

+

Well if you don't be believing me, then why do you come around?

--

For entertainment. I never know what's coming out of your mouth next. Anyway, why didn't you drive for Ced?

+

Those monkeys stressed me out. I'm scared of them Bro.

I trusted my street instincts and went to Sizzler instead, then my phone started blowing up.

Canary Park

\-\-

I thought you hooked up with Alexis?

\+

(pausing to respond) Oh yea ... .I did, but that was AFTER we went to Sizzler. I put that on my mama.

\-\-

Your lies are so stupid.

They don't make sense.

For why, huh? For why?

You don't even have a car.

\+

I do have a car.

—

Then why are we always walking, taking the bus or ubering? For why?

And why would Ced ask you to drive when he has his own car?

Answer that. For why?

Canary Park

+

What are you, a detective now?

—

Ced hustled with dice games in middle school. Used to break everybody's pockets. His grandfather found out and shut him down. **(pacing, thinking, stressing while absorbing the news)**

Man…. I can't trust you. You always making something up. I have to find out for myself.

Hold on. **(he calls a friend.)**

Yo! Bro did you hear anything about Ced getting arrested?

Are you serious?

Ced?

When?

Unbelievable!

Alright. I'll talk to you later. **(he hangs up)**

I never thought that Ced would get arrested for anything.

Canary Park

+

Told you. He had everybody fooled thinking he was Mr. Fabuloso. It's the quiet ones you have to watch out for.

--

I still don't believe it. That's my guy. We both were team captains.

+

You're in denial. That's what happens when you put people on a pedestal, they let you down.

--

You're just a hater. There has to be more to this.

+

He did something to get arrested. I know that much.

(They exit. Junebug follows. Ced enters deep in thought. He sits at a bench. Fatimah follows a few steps behind, giving him space. There's

heavy tension in the air as they move in silence. Ced sits down, clearly stressed out and Fatimah sits behind him, humming while massaging his shoulders and neck, doing her best to comfort him. She sits beside him, holding his hand.)

Fatimah

Everything will be alright. Do you need anything?

Ced

I have a killer migraine and I'm exhausted.

Fatimah

That's from the stress Ced, We need you to stay positive.

(Ced takes a deep breath and massages his temples. Fatimah continues massaging his neck.)

So now that you're out on bail, what're you going to do?

Ced

I don't know Tima.

Canary Park

Fatimah

What do you mean you don't know? Tell the truth.

Ced

I ain't no snitch.

Fatimah

Are you serious right now, Ced?

Ced

People get killed for snitching. Don't you get it Tima?

Fatimah

YG is a snake. That was his stash in your car.

Ced

It's not that easy Tima.

Fatimah

It is that easy Ced.

Ced

Canary Park

You think it's easy. That's because you're on the outside looking in. No one will believe that bag wasn't mine and I had never seen that bag before.

Fatimah

You owe it to me and your son to be with us. Why are you trying to save YG? He doesn't give a damn about you or anyone but himself.

Ced

He's a friend.

Fatimah

A friend?! **(sarcastically laughing)** You're his friend. He doesn't feel the same way about you.

Ced

You just don't abandon people like that. This is real. **(shows his foot)** I'm wearing an ankle bracelet. My trial is in a few months.

Fatimah

Don't you think I know this?

Ced

Canary Park

I have enough on my head. I just spent a week in jail. Missed that job orientation. Can't eat or sleep. May not get a chance to walk across the stage.

Fatimah

You're not alone. This affects all of us. I'm here for you.

Ced

If they try me as an adult, I'm looking at 10-15 years…. NOT you. At least after I come home I can hold my head up. You ain't heard? Snitches get stitches.

Fatimah

How do you sound? You're willing to give up years of your life for some childish snitches get snitches nursery rhyme?

Ced

You think that I want to leave you and CJ? If I go to jail or if I snitch, either way I'm done.

Fatimah

We can talk about this...if there's a will, there's a way Baby.

Ced

I don't want to talk...My head is about to explode from all this talking and thinking. Leave it alone. Please.

Fatimah

Baby listen. We could.....

Ced

(exploding) Just shut up already! You doing too much. You're like a hammer **(rising and frustrated, swinging his arms.)** constantly pounding my skull in with question after question. Give me some space to breathe!

Fatimah

(shocked for a moment, she walks off thinking, then turns back to Ced, emotionally.)

Sounds like you've made your decision. Well let me tell you mine. Trust and believe. I'm not going to be one of those women traveling 2-3 hours every weekend with your baby looking at you through three inches of glass. I'm not running up my phone bill accepting collect calls and busting my butt to put money on your books. I've always loved your loyalty. Now that same loyalty got you caught up.

Ced

(rises slowly clapping his hands and gives her a standing ovation.) Bravo! Bravo! Encore! You deserve a Toney Award for that performance. How long have you been practicing that speech? Probably since I was locked up. I thought I could trust you to be here. This is how you do me?

Fatimah

I don't see anything heroic about ruining your life for something you didn't do.

What about the military? Are you going to throw away your dreams of being a pilot also?

Ced

This is a felony charge. It already messed up my chances for the Air Force.

Fatimah

Canary Park

Then fight for it. Fight for us! Go to school. You have a bunch of scholarship offers.

<u>Ced</u>

Soon as those schools hear about a gun and drug charge, I'm done.

<u>Fatimah</u>

You have an excuse for everything.

<u>Ced</u>

I'm trying Tima! What you want me to do?

<u>Fatimah</u>

Stop accepting what you don't deserve.

<u>Ced</u>

I thought you would understand. We have a child together.

<u>Fatimah</u>

Exactly!

<u>Ced</u>

Then wait for me. Hold me down.

Canary Park

Fatimah

(standing, holding his hands, then his face) We'll both be prisoners. You in jail, and me putting my life on hold while you earn your street cred. We're supposed to be breaking generational curses. You know my mom and aunties went through this. Jail changes men. Only a few return with a plan and follow through with it. Most of them who come home either choose another woman or go right back in. Institutionalized. This.... Us.... Under these conditions.... For YG???? **(shaking her head, then the rest of her body to make a definitive statement.)** Not going to happen Ced. I already know the outcome.

Ced

(moves her hands from off of him) Fine! I don't need you! Like YG said, can't trust women. Why don't you go get with him? I see the way he looks at you. You two probably planned this whole thing to get me out the way. We are over! Best believe, I'll get my son when I come back home.

Fatimah

That's what you think of me? Ced? You're breaking up with me?

Ced

Get out of my face. Go somewhere. You disgust me.

(She is completely broken by his words.

She walks off and collapses into Pops' arms as he enters.

Fatimah and Pops pantomime her encounter with Ced before she breaks down again into his arms.

He hugs her, wipes her tears, and gives her words of encouragement, then watches her walk off stage before turning around towards Ced, who is deep in thought, feeling sorry for himself and is oblivious to Pops' presence.)

Pops

Son.

Ced

Pops.

Canary Park

Pops

Just ran into Fatimah...**(staring silently, thinking, then sits next to Ced on the bench.)** She's a good woman Ced.

Ced

Not you too Pops! **(jumping up and exploding)** I don't want to hear it!

Pops

(his authoritative voice momentarily snaps Ced out of his vibe.) I put our home up for your bail, so you are going to listen!

(Grabs him Ced by his shoulders) Breathe slowly. Calm yourself down..... **(Pops and Ced take in a few deep breaths until Ced regains his composure.)** You are pushing a good woman away, Ced. A man only gets one or two of them in a lifetime. She's scared. You have to give her security. She deserves that.

Ced

What about my security? What about my peace?

Pops

Canary Park

It's no longer just about you. You have a family.

Ced

I'm scared Pops. What did I do to deserve this?

Pops

I understand. This is life and sometimes Son, when you are just about to achieve your goal, life throws you a changeup, some adversity to see how much you really want it. It's testing your strength and belief systems.

Ced

Good ole adversity....You always said that Pops.

Pops

Well here it is. **(spreads his arms wide)** Now tell me. How bad do you want your freedom, your dreams, your family? **(gets in Ced's face, foreheads touching while clapping his hands.)** Get your mind right. Think positive. Respond without reacting.

Ced

(Ced gets himself together, pacing nervously. He takes a few more deep breaths to calm

himself.) The lawyer called earlier and wants me to consider a plea bargain. He said it was a good deal. If I plead guilty, they'll reduce my sentence. I'm thinking about it.

Pops

The hell you will! You are innocent. No plea deal. They'll own you for the rest of your life. No son. I raised you to man up, not to man down. We'll find a new lawyer.

Ced

It was YG's bag.

Pops

I figured that. Now tell me again, everything from the start to finish.

Ced

I gave YG a ride even though my instincts told me not to. He picked up a package, said it was for a job. I dropped him back off here. That was it. When I saw him talking to RayRay, I got this feeling. YG has been trying to prove himself for years. I guess he used me for his initiation or something.

Pops

Don't blame yourself for helping people. Your heart was in the right place, his was not. Now you know. (**thinking; processing**) RayRay. That's Wells' grandson. Yeah you guys played little league together. You two were close. What happened?

Ced

Nothing really. After his moms got sick, he was about making money. He quit school and did his thing fulltime to support them.

Pops

That's a tough spot for a young man to be in. Now what happened after you dropped YG back here?

Ced

(sits as if he is driving with his hand on the steering wheel and gives the perspective from the traffic stop.) I was about to drop off food and pampers for CJ. Cops had a check point, literally a few doors from Tima's house. He asked for my licence and registration. I gave it to him. He looks in the seat and asks if he could check my backpack and I'm like yea. I had nothing to hide. Then he pulled out guns, a stack of money and drugs. I told them I had never seen that bag before. The cop said, "that's what they all say."

I remembered to keep my mouth shut like you taught me. He made me get out of the car, handcuffed me and read me my rights, and put me in the back of his patrol car. More cops came out of nowhere and searched the car.

Pops

You've never been in trouble, and those cops violated your rights. Your supervisor, recruiting officer, teachers and coaches vouched and wrote character reference letters on your behalf. You have to tell the police exactly what happened. Where's YG now?

Ced

Nobody has seen or heard him since I was arrested.

Canary Park

Pops

We'll figure this out, Son. YG seems to be reckless and impulsive. RayRay is the more grounded one. We can reason with him.

Ced

If I snitch on YG, it will bring attention to RayRay. They always want the leader to be brought down. That's a whole different beast right there. We got family here and if he doesn't get to me, he'll get to you and Fatimah. I can't risk that Pops. I ain't no snitch.

Pops

You young people kill me with that snitch stuff, you all a bunch of cowards.

Ced

How am I a coward? I'm trying to protect you. RayRay has a rep.

Pop

(yelling, throws his hat down.) I don't need your protection! You think we didn't have gangs when I was coming up? YG and RayRay are cancers.

They hold our community hostage with drugs and violence. Everyone is afraid of them. Since you don't want to tell on him and put him in jail, then you have to put the fear of God in him so he won't hurt anyone else. If that doesn't work, then you make him disappear! By any means.............Yea I said it. Either way, if you don't do anything about it, then you're just as guilty as the one committing the crime.

Ced

Times have changed Pops.

Pops

It sure has. If someone harms Fatimah and CJ, you telling me that you won't want to find out who did it? You're going to accept that snitch rule then, huh? You protect your family by taking the monsters off the streets.

(Ced turns away and is about to leave when Pop grabs his arm and pulls him back)

I'm talking to you boy, don't you turn your back on me! **(Pops grabs him by the shoulders.)** Our daughter, your **(gets emotional)** passed away when you were still a baby. We promised her to take care of you. Your father was never any help. In and out of jail, on and off drugs. You have resentment towards him that you can't even begin to understand yet. That's where your focus and ambition comes from. Trying to be a bigger man than him. Now you're going to end up in the same place he's at. For what? I can't let you flush all your hard work down the toilet?

(Ced faces Pops and breaks down. He finally lets all his emotions out. Pops holds him tight until he releases.)

Pops

Get it all out Son.

Ced

I don't know what to do.

Pops

We're family, Son. Come on. Let's go home. We'll figure it out. **(they exit in each other's arms.)**

Canary Park

ACT II

Canary Park

Act 2 Scene 1

(Junebug walks on stage with his shopping cart.

He finds bottles and cans in the trash,

money on the ground,

sits on the bench and takes out a portable radio to play music.

He searches for stations until he finds the perfect song.

Satisfied,

Junebug takes out a hand sanitizer bottle to clean his hands,

puts a rag in his collar as a bib,

Takes a sandwich from his pocket,

unwraps it and eats while nodding to the beat in total happiness.

After he finishes his meal,

Junebug rises,

Canary Park

carefully dusts himself off and throws away his trash.

He looks for a comfortable spot,

lays down his blanket,

yawns, stretches and goes to sleep.)

Chorus

Male and woman

\+

Guess what. I have news for you. You will never believe this!

\--

What? Spill the tea.

\+

Ced and Fatimah broke up.

\--

No way, they've been together forever. When?

\+

About a week ago.

Canary Park

\--

I feel like I'm going through a divorce myself just from hearing this news.... That's terrible.

\+

But listen to this, **(looks around as if his news is top secret)......(dramatic pause)** Fatimah is doing.........**(falls on the floor).....** YG.

\--

Nooooooooo! **(she covers her mouth as if she's about to vomit, then falls dramatically.)**

\+

Saw them together at the mall. He bought her Mrs. Fields.... It's official.

–

Ewww-**(takes out her asthma inhaler and takes 2 breaths)** How do you go from Ced to YG? She was supposed to level up. That's like going from a Mercedes to a skate board. **(rubs her temple in disbelief)**

When I tell my girl, she is going to go off.

Canary Park

\+

Get locked up and your girl starts seeing one of your boys.

−

Scandalous. She must be desperate for someone to provide for CJ.

\+

That's why I don't trust women.

− −

No women don't respect you, that's why you don't trust them.

\+

See you didn't even have to go there. That's messed up that you would even bring something like that up.

—

Well it's true.

\+

No it's not. I just chose the wrong ones.

Canary Park

—

Now, we can agree on that. Plus you are too nice. Stop being a pushover.

+

I am not a pushover.

--

(sticks her hand out) You got $5?

+

(goes into his wallet and takes out money) Here you go.

--

See ….That's exactly what I'm talking about.

+

I don't get it. We're friends. You need it, I have it.

—

Here's your money….**(attempting to give it back)**

+

Canary Park

(refusing it, she shrugs and puts it in her pocket.) You don't need it?

\--

No, I don't. I was proving a point. You can't say yes to everyone, all the time.

They will take you for granted.

++

So how do I know who I should help?

\--

Pay attention to the one who likes you, not the one who you're chasing. Sometimes the one who's really down for you is right there in front of your eyes. Just have to pay attention.....**(she smiles and walks off. He pauses for a moment, looks at the audience, then it finally dawns on him. He runs off to catch her.)**

(Fatimah makes her entrance.

She takes a deep breath,

sits on the bench,

opens her purse and takes out a mirror

Canary Park

to adjust her makeup,

fixes her hair, and sprays on perfume.

Satisfied with her appearance,

She practices a few seductive seated positions on the park bench as if she's anxiously expecting someone.

From the shadows, YG emerges.)

YG

Hey Fatimah.

Fatimah

Hey YG. Thanks for coming around **(She stands up and gives him a hug.)**

YG

You smell delicious.....like a churro.

Fatimah

Thank you.

YG

(Circling Tima while taking in deep breaths of her scent.)

I knew you would call.

<u>Fatimah</u>

You knew I would call? How?

<u>YG</u>

It's our time... Sup Baby?

Are you feeling better?

<u>Fatimah</u>

I am. Thanks for being there for me. I can't believe we talked for 2 hours last night. My phone almost died twice.

<u>YG</u>

Picture me not being there for you. Remember, I knew you before you met Ced.

<u>Fatimah</u>

I'm so disappointed in Ced. He's not the man I thought he was.

<u>YG</u>

I told you from 1st grade Fatimah. **(flexing)** I'm the man.

Canary Park

Fatimah

(**Submitting**) Yes you are. You can call me Tima...If you want to.

YG

(**feeling himself**) Well you can call me Yafe...If you want to.

Fatimah

Ya what?

YG

Yafe- (**spells it**) Y-a-f-e It sounds like Ya-f-a-y. Yafe.

Fatimah

Yafe. All this time, I never knew that was your real name.

What does it mean?

YG

It means handsome. My Grandmother named me.

Fatimah

That's the perfect name. It fits you.

YG

Tima, girl you flirting with me?

Fatimah

What are you gonna do about it Yafe? You already know.

YG

Girl….Don't play with me girl. I'll eat you up like a carne asada wet burrito. We'll have a bunch of little taco babies running around here playing with chips and salsa.

Fatimah

(laughing) Oh my God. You are so silly. … And, you really have a thing for Mexican food. Yaf **(stutters trying to pronounce his name)**

YG

Ya-fe. Call me YG if it's easier. And yes, I love Mexican food.

Fatimah

Canary Park

I like Yafe. It has a beautiful sound. It'll take me a while until I get used to it.

So what's up YG **(flirtatiously laughing)** I mean…. Yafe

Yafe, Yafe? Tell me something though….

YG

What up?

Fatimah

Why do you always have to be the bad boy? You have a great personality. Funny. You have me cracking up all the time. People don't know how cool you really are. Seems like you enjoy being the villain.

YG

That's what I do well. People don't respect good guys, especially women. That's why you're here right now with me. **(opens his backpack to find his water. Takes a drink and puts it back in his bag).**

Am I lying?

Fatimah

That was one of the realest things I ever heard.

(laughs uncomfortably)

Not sure how I'm supposed to respond to that. **(fixes her hair and puts on lip gloss.)**

Here comes that awkward silence.

YG

I'm used to people betraying me. I protect myself by betraying them first. The only person I trust is my grandmother. It is what it is.

Fatimah

That's so sad. **(holds his hand)** Well, let's make a promise that we'll be straight up with each other moving forward. No secrets. You can trust me. Yafe.

YG

I've been waiting a long time to hear that from you. Tima. Thank you.

I've always loved you.

Fatimah

For real YG?

Canary Park

YG

Yeah I want the whole world to know.

Fatimah

About to record you so I can always remember this moment.

YG

Do it! **(YG shows an uncharacteristic vulnerable side and stands up with his hands open wide, shouting)** Show this to our future babies. I have always loved you Tima, and always will!

Fatima

Funny how relationships just fall into place, unexpectedly. I gave my everything to Ced. Now I'm sitting here with you.

YG

We can talk about romance later. Right now, let's get down to business. You got that money?

Fatimah

Yes I have it. I still don't understand why you need $3,000 from me.

Canary Park

YG

You want to be with me, there's a fee. **(laughing)** No, I'm just kidding. On God. You will get it back, with interest.

Fatimah

Okay **(she hands him an envelope. He opens and counts the money, then puts the envelope in his pocket.)** I hope this helps.

YG

Look, RayRay will be here in a few. I need you to be quiet and stay out of the way when he shows up. I'll explain everything to you later.

(RayRay enters and walks directly between Fatimah and a YG. YG moves back. RayRay stands in the middle, studying both of them.)

RayRay

You good, Fatimah?

Fatimah

I'm good RayRay. **(she looks around as if ashamed.)**

Canary Park

RayRay

How's Ced?

Fatimah

I don't know how he is. **(takes a deep uneasy breath)** Ced broke up with me.

RayRay

Sorry to hear that.

(disappointed by the news he shakes his head, then focuses on YG, grabs him by the arm and walks him a few steps away from Fatimah)

You got my work?

YG

(motions to Fatimah) Go take a walk Tima, this is men's business.

(Fatimah obeys, walks away and takes out her phone to keep herself occupied.)

(to RayRay) RayRay what's up my brother? Long time no see. **(hands him the envelope.)**

RayRay

Canary Park

You got a lot of nerve showing your face around here. **(checks the envelope and counts the money.)** This is kind of light.

YG

How? I owed you 3 racks. It's all there. Count it.

RayRay

I'm collecting interest, for the inconvenience.

YG

All I have is $1500 from my side hustle.

RayRay

(pocket checks YG, takes off his backpack, finds his money, counts it and puts it in his pocket.)

This'll work.

YG

That's all I have RayRay.

RayRay

Ask me if I care?

YG

Canary Park

Was you really going to shoot me?

RayRay

I still want to pop you... I told you to leave Ced out of it and you made it hot around here for everyone.

YG

(nonchalantly)

He ain't talked. We good in the hood

Ced's out on bail. I heard he's taking a plea. They found the guns on him, not you or me.

Ha **(laughing)** I got bars!

RayRay

Lower your voice, fool. You talk too much.

YG

(animated stage whisper) I put in work for you.

RayRay

(stage whisper) Work? You messed up a simple drop off. Got Ced arrested and **(looking around**

at Fatimah) You trifling for trying to get at his girl. You foul.

YG

Bro…. I'm trying to get put on and get this money, not sign up for jury duty. Besides, she called me. She knows I always had a thing for her, but she couldn't show feelings cause she was with Ced. Now he's about to be out of the picture, **(pounding his chest)** she wants me.

RayRay

You don't respect rank, rules or loyalty. I told you not to bring meth into the neighborhood and you didn't listen. You're a liability.

YG

Oh so you a gangster with morals? **(laughs sarcastically)** Give me break RayRay. You don't know what I can bring to the table.

RayRay

Hell no. Straight up. I don't like you. I don't trust you and if I see or hear you claiming anything, or selling that meth around here or anything else without my say, there's a few hot ones with your name on it. On sight.

(he pushes YG out of his way and exits, leaving YG embarrassed and confused. YG has another temper tantrum before controlling himself. Fatimah has observed everything.)

YG

Tima! Come here girl.

(Fatimah walks over) Is everything okay YG?

YG

Yeah. **(nervous)** Look…. You have a car right? Let's get on the road. We need to leave LA tonight.

Fatimah

Yes, I do have a car, but why do we have to leave LA? This is my home and…you know I'm not alone.

YG

What're you talking about?

Fatimah

I'm a mother. We have a son.

YG

We...................? As in ....me?

Or Oui like you speak French.

Fatimah

CJ needs a father especially since Ced is about to plead guilty.

YG

(irritated) Leave that lil bastard with your mother. What I look like taking care of another man's kid?... Matter of fact, don't even bring up his name again. Must of lost your mind talking about CJ needs a father.

Fatimah

You're expecting me to abandon my child for you and just pick up and leave with you tonight?

YG

(gets in her face) Did I stutter? We starting fresh. You can come back and visit him on your own time.

Canary Park

Fatimah

(thinking, surprised by YG's aggression, she attempts to calm him down.) Okay baby...I'm sorry to upset you. Anything you say. Please, Yafe. I'm sorry.

YG

Yeah that's more like it. Like I said, we need to leave the city tonight.

Fatimah

Why do we have to leave YG?

You're asking for so much, too soon. I need to be near my family.

YG

Woman, you ask too many questions. Just do as you're told.

Ced didn't discipline you to shut your mouth or stay in your place. Huh?

Fatimah

Stay in my place? **(she turns her back to YG, takes a deep frustrating breath and prays** silently, before continuing.) What about school? I'm a month from graduation and was already accepted to the school of my dreams.

YG

Ain't no one got time for that school. You don't need an education when you have me. You looking for something to do, study my needs.

Fatimah

Wow. You're so insecure. I need something to have of my own. How're you going to take care of me? You already have my life savings and now you want me to leave CJ.

YG

(he grabs her by the collar and forces her to sit down on the bench)

I told you not to say that name.

(YG turns his back. She fixes her clothes, wipes away her tears, stands behind YG and hesitantly rubs his shoulders until he turns around and holds her around her waist.)

Fatimah

Canary Park

I'm sorry. I deserved that YG. I promise... I'll never mention my son's name again.

YG

That's right. Make it easy on yourself.

(Fatimah circles the bench before sitting down in front of YG. He's feeling a power rush that's building his ego to a dangerous level.

He opens up his backpack and takes another drink of water, then puts it back in his bag)

Fatimah

Ced was getting his hustle on huh baby, he was showing you how to get it done so you can be like him?

YG

(arrogantly feeling disrespected. Strutting using aggressive motion to express himself.) Whaaat? Woman please! Ced showing me about these streets? Ha! That's a joke. He's not built for this hustle game. **(proudly announcing)** I was moving guns for RayRay, made the drop and picked up the cash, plus did a side hustle on my own with meth. I needed Ced to give me a ride... I f-ed up and took the wrong backpack. That $3000 you gave me was to get RayRay off my bumper. I owed him for the guns.

Fatimah

Now how are you going to take care of me? No car? Where's your money coming from? Do you even have your own place to stay?

YG

Relax. I kept the connect. Javier on the Eastside. He supplies the guns and RayRay sells them. Javi runs a methlab too, but that's another story. RayRay was moving 20 guns a week for like $500-$1,000 each. I'll double his hustle. You know me...I'm a fast learner. I'll be running my own business after I eliminate RayRay. **(thinking)** Look, let's get out of here, go to a new city and have a fresh start. That meth would have made me $20gs on the streets. I'm in a hole now. I owe Javi for that too. Gotta find a way to re-up. We are going to stay with my Grandmother in Vegas and lay low until I get back on my feet.

Canary Park

Fatimah

Vegas? You mean you're broke?

YG

Not completely. I have jewelry to pawn. It's worth a few thousand dollars.

Fatimah

So it is true. You really stole a jewelry box from the twin's house that belonged to their mom? They've been looking for you. Aren't you scared for your life?

YG

Ain't nobody thinking about the twins or their mama.

Fatimah

Their mother passed away last summer. How can you be so insensitive?

YG

So then, she won't be needing her jewelry. Will she? **(laughs sarcastically and shrugs his shoulders)** Can't take it with ya.

Canary Park

Fatimah

No car. No job? No place of your own? No respect? A thief.

(she starts laughing which turns into crying, clapping her hands and slapping her knees.)

YG

What's so funny Tima?

Fatimah
You're such an idiot.

YG

Excuse me? **(he looks around the park under benches, in the trash, his armpits, bottom of his shoes, up in the sky and on the ground.)**

Fatimah

What are you looking for YG?

YG

I'm looking to see who you think you talking to…. Heffa.

Fatimah

Canary Park

You already know. I'm talking to you Yafe.... .You sorry, pathetic excuse for a man.

YG

Whoooooaaa. Are you bi-polar? Every turn into someone brand new.

First you lead me on.

Then you betray me by getting with Ced.

Ignore me all these years.

As of last night, you want me back.

Now you just insulted me.

What medications are you on?

Girl. You need counseling.

You Craycray.

For real.

(Pops enters and walks over to Fatima)

Pops

Good evening.

Fatimah

Pops! **(they hug. YG is intimidated by their connection and wonders what is going on. He circles them trying to figure it out.)**

Pops

How are you doing Baby Girl? How's the little man doing?

Fatimah

I could be better, you know. CJ **(she looks at YG and rolls her eyes)** CJ is getting big.

Pops

Make sure you tell your mom I enjoyed her lasagna. I ate the whole batch in one sitting.

Fatimah

Yea we all love Mama's cooking. She'll be happy to know you enjoyed it too.

YG

Yo. Hello! **(spreading his arms and jumping to get attention)** Ya'll rude. You don't see me standing here?

Canary Park

(still getting ignored, YG walks up to Pops and taps his shoulder) Excuse me..... Mr. Somebody's Grandpa...Me and my woman were having a conversation and you're interrupting our flow. I'd appreciate it if....

Pops

Get out of my face before I choke the evil out of you.

(YG backs up, begins to look around while whispering to himself.)

Pops

(To Fatima) What's wrong with this boy?

Fatimah

He's looking around to see who you're talking to.

Pops

Well wherever you found him, please take him back.

(Fatimah turns around and walks away.)

YG

Hey, where you think you going?

Canary Park

Come here woman!!!

Tima! We have plans.

Fatimah

This isn't going to work out, Yafe. We're on two different levels. But, you already knew this.

(Pops stands between them as Fatimah walks off stage. Pops and YG stare down each other until Pops turns around and walks off. YG stands there alone, defeated. He sits on the bench, takes a towel from his bag and covers his head, trying to conceal his tears of disappointment. He emotionally addresses the audience.)

Once again I'm betrayed, and ya'll wonder why I look out for myself. Tell you something, that's the last time I put my trust in anyone. All of you are liars! Every last one of you! **(he kicks over the trashcan on his way off stage.)**

(Junebug wakes up from the commotion.

Canary Park

He stands up the garbage can and throws away the discarded trash, and sits down on the bench.

He starts laughing, a laugh so good to him that he can't breathe.

The laughter then turns into tears.

He holds his head in his hands and weeps a violent shaking cry.

He takes out a rag,

wipes his tears,

the bench

and around the rim of the trashcan,

Then the ground.

He returns to his spot and lies back down. Moments later the twins rush on stage in synchronized movement. Again, their timing is imperfect and they show disappointment that they missed YG)

Canary Park

Act 2 Scene 2

(Pop enters the scene. He sits at the park bench, unpacks his chess set, sets up the pieces and begins playing a game of chess by himself. RayRay enters. RayRay looks around impatiently checking the time. Pops and RayRay make eye contact and acknowledge each other. Pops refocuses on his game, makes a few more moves while RayRay waits.)

Pops

Do you play chess?

RayRay

Not anymore.

Pops

Why not?

RayRay

I don't have the time.

Pops

Is your name RayRay?

Canary Park

RayRay

(he turns around, curious-stares at Pops) You know me?

Pops

I do. **(continues studying his chess game)** Knew you when you were a little kid playing sports. Come over here RayRay. I'm the one who arranged the meeting.

RayRay

How you know me?

Pops

I'm Ced's Grandfather.

RayRay

So....What does that have to do with me?

Pops

I have a business opportunity for you.

RayRay

(laughing) Okay this sounds interesting. What's the business opportunity you have for me?

Canary Park

Pops

You have two hours to pack up and get out of town, go to jail or....

RayRay

Or what? **(he raises his voice, body language hardens and is ready for confrontation.)** This doesn't sound like a business opportunity. Sounds like a threat. I don't take threats from nobody.

Pops

(chuckles while focusing on his game) All that bravado. All that testosterone built up. It must have convinced you that everybody is supposed to be scared when you puff up. Tell me, Son. What happens when you meet people who're not scared of you?

RayRay

You are wasting my time, old man. If anyone is leaving, it's going to be you.

Pops

Canary Park

I have something for you to listen to. Then we can get down to business.

RayRay

(Agitated) What are you talking about?

Pops

Relax. **(he demonstrates by taking a few deep breaths)** Breathe. **(takes out a phone, searching for something while RayRay grows impatient)** Patience never hurts anyone. Everyone is always in a rush. Here it is. Found the file I was looking for. Are you ready?

(he plays a recording)

" Whaaat? Woman please. *Ced teaching me about these streets? Ha! That's a joke Tima. He don't have the hustle game in him. I was moving guns for RayRay, made the drop and picked up the cash, plus did a side hustle on my own with some meth. I just needed Ced to give me a ride... I f-ed up and took the wrong backpack. That $3000 you gave me was to get RayRay off my bumper. I owed him for the guns...*"

Canary Park

Fatimah

Now how are you going to take care of me? Where's your money coming from? Where are we going to stay? Do you even have your own place to stay?

(RayRay's body starts to implode. He can't believe what he is hearing.)

YG

Relax. I kept the connect, Javier, on the east side. He supplies the guns and RayRay sells them. Javi runs a methlab too, but that's another story. RayRay was selling 50 guns a week for like $500-$1,000 each. I'll double his hustle. You know me...I'm a fast learner. I'll be running my own business after I eliminate RayRay.

RayRay

Eliminate RayRay? **(gets up and moves around, trying not to show how worried he is)** .... So you have a recording of some rat running his mouth. That's not enough to prove that I committed a crime.

Pops

Canary Park

There's more incriminating information before and after that clip. Gave you just a little taste to wet your appetite. **(puts the phone away and continues with his chess game giving RayRay time to process)** You used to be a good kid, never thought you would grow up to poison your own community. What happened to you?

RayRay

You think I'm stupid? You trying to record me to say anything that'll get me in jail. Not me! You don't have permission to record me.

Pops

(rises and opens up his clothes to show he doesn't have a wire on him.)

No wire RayRay. I'm not working with the feds.

RayRay

You want to play this game with me...Old man.

Pops

I've lived in this community long before your parents were born. This is my home... I'm going to protect what's mine.

RayRay

(Angrily) So am I!

Pops

I can't have you destroying this community. One way or the other, you're leaving.

RayRay

I'm not going anywhere Old Man. **(Looks around and attempts to take out his weapon. Junebug springs into action behind RayRay who does not see him coming. He holds RayRay in a chokehold from behind with his own weapon aimed at RayRay's back.**

Junebug

Lets get it on! I got your old man right here, you young punk. I've been gatekeeping longer than you've been alive. I wish you would. I'll remove your soul from your body.

Pops

Chillout RayRay. Put the gun down....Listen. No one needs to get hurt.

Canary Park

(Junebug takes RayRay's gun from his waist and pushes him away downstage.)

Junebug

Move slowly and don't be eyeballing me with your two first names having ass.

Pops

Sit down, Son. You don't want to aggravate, Junebug. He doesn't have much patience.

RayRay

Hell no. I ain't sitting down. Do what you came to do.

Pops

Suit yourself.

(Pops then takes out a sheet of paper from his pocket, adjusts his glasses and begins reading.)

-You live at 1306 Imperial Blvd Apt. 1206.

-Your mother, Asia lives in Lancaster with your twin sisters. Her address is 24 Ryan Lane.

–She's on disability. Your twin sisters Myia and Mia attend Clyde Elementary, both in the 4th grade.

–Your girlfriend, Shay Rivers is 3 months pregnant and she lives on 103rd and Crenshaw with her mother and little brother.

–Shay drives a 2018 Silver Chevy Impala registered in your name. Rayshawn Jackson. The personalized license plate is "SHAYRAY."

I pray that won't be the name of your child.

–Your grandfather is Jim Wells and he lives at 8300 West Blvd.

–You use his garage as one of your stash houses.

–Public Storage unit 55E in Culver City.

–Your license number is C0976652.

–Social security # 626 78 2312.

(Pops hands the paper to RayRay, who reads it in disbelief)

You keep that, I have copies spread out. If you turn the paper over, you'll see that I have the same information on your next two commanders in line.

Junebug

(laughs a satisfying laugh)

Got em!

(RayRay turns the page over, reads, then crumples it and throws it down. Junebug motions for him to pick up his trash and put it in his pocket.)

(RayRay sits down clearly defeated, rubbing his head.)

Pops

This is the business plan I am proposing. Get out of town or go to jail.

Junebug

Or I end you.

RayRay

How did ... .Who told you?

Junebug

Canary Park

You all sing like a bunch of canaries waiting to be sacrificed. Tell all business while on your speakerphones and think no one is watching or listening. Then you get the nerve to act shocked when people know your moves. We used to call that dry snitching. You underestimated me and exposed yourselves.

Pops

If anything happens to me, my family, or my property RayRay, you better hope that the cops get to you before my people do. There's a few contracts out just in case you want to prove you want to step outside yourself. The last thing you want is a team of old gatekeepers hunting you down.

Junebug

You letting this young fool off the hook? People like him don't change.

Pops

We'll see Junebug. He's still young. His brain isn't even fully developed yet. Besides I can see it in his eyes. He wants out, but doesn't know how.

Canary Park

Junebug

I know that's right, but that's what makes him dangerous.

RayRay

I didn't want to get Ced involved.

Pops

Neither did I, but it happened and my grandson is facing hard time. He's innocent.

RayRay

What're you going to with that recording?

Pops

Our lawyers have it. It's more than enough evidence to prove Ced's innocence. They'll drop the case.

RayRay

Yeah but they'll go after YG. He'll rat me out.

He ain't built for jail. All I did was move weapons. He's putting drugs on the streets.

Pops

Canary Park

Both of you are worse than oppressors. When those guns and drugs come into our community, the only people who get hurt are ones who look like us. Your own people. You are both so consumed with your profits that you can't see how it's destroying lives.

RayRay

We have to eat too. How else are we supposed to survive?

Pops

Earn it. You have choices. Figure it out. **(Pop finishes his game, packs up his pieces and leaves with Junebug. RayRay sits by himself, thinking, takes out his phone and sends a few texts, gets up and leaves. Lights fade to black.)**

Canary Park

Act 2 Scene 3

(It's a few weeks later. Two people jog into the park, stop to rest and begin stretching. They converse in between catching their breaths.)

Chorus:

--

That was a long run. What's up with you?

+

I had to burn some steam off.

--

You were moving.

+

Just a lot going on.

--

Why, what's going on?

+

Did you hear about YG?

--

Canary Park

What happened?

+

(Stretching slowly, taking deep breaths, looking away for a few seconds and wiping sweat or tears.)

They found him at the beach.

Two bullets in the chest and two in the head.

--

Damn-they did him like that? Why?

+

You know YG, always active and running his mouth. Looks like it finally caught up with him.

--

You think RayRay got him?

+

Who knows? YG was shady. Made enemies everywhere he went.

--

Canary Park

I was not expecting you to tell me that YG is dead.

+

Crazy, huh. Heard that he was recorded giving names in a federal case.

The twins were looking for him too. He stole something that belonged to their mother.

--

Sounds like the twins got to him. That's that street life he was always claiming. His funeral is on Saturday.

+

How old was he?

--

He turned 18 this year. Same age as us.

+

That's too soon to die.

--

He was a jerk, but it's still messed up.

Canary Park

+

True

--

You going to his funeral?

+

I doubt it. Sounds mean, but he wasn't a guy who let you get close to him. I've known YG since the 3rd grade. I barely knew him and from what I did know, I didn't like. He didn't care about anybody.

--

So why is it bothering us?

+

I care because it's another young brother who didn't get a chance to live.

I didn't expect to feel this way.

--

That was YG.

Complicated.

Canary Park

(they sit for a moment in silence absorbing the news.)

+

Maybe I'll go to the funeral.

--

Why?

+

Cause at the end of the day, we're all we have. Whatever made him like that....I hope he's in a good place.

--

Maybe I'll go with you.

(they exit)

Canary Park

Act 2 Scene 3

(Pops arrives, alone and sits on the bench. From his bag he unwraps two small urns. He places one on either side of him, sits back and spreads out his arms on the bench. He picks up an urn, hugs and caresses it, then speaks to it.)

My precious Love. Our grandson graduated yesterday. I felt your presence all day. **(Pops begins to cry. Wipes his tears. Walks with the urn in his hand as if he's holding hands with someone.)** Yes, these are finally tears of joy. Finally. I didn't know how I was going to raise him after you left. It's been hard, I miss you so much.

Ced made it. We made it. We weathered the storm. Now he's shining. He's just like you. He has your heart, such a giver and smart too, has your intelligence. Well, you know that. You raised him too. I'm so proud of him. He constantly exceeds my expectations. He's a leader and such a hard worker. He got that from me. **(chuckles)** I hope you are pleased. Couldn't have done this without you. How are you doing? What's it like in heaven, same as it is on Earth? I

Canary Park

hope you are at peace and with Jessica. I miss you both. Never thought it would be you to go first. But, like you always said, we plan and God smiles. **(rotates his ring on his finger and takes it off and puts it back on.)** I think I am ready to finally move forward with my life. See what the world has to offer. Ced is a man now. He's about to get married. He has a good woman in Fatimah. I'm so, so happy for him. They have the type of love that we shared. As for me **(playing with his ring)** I don't want to be alone anymore. About to find me a new friend. Not to replace you. That's impossible. Felt you should know that I'm moving forward in life. Feels like I've been standing still too long. I need to go somewhere, do something, with someone by my side. I'll always love you.

(Pops puts his wife's urn on the bench carefully before he gently holds the other one, which belongs to his daughter. He holds it against his heart, kisses it, then sits it on his lap.)

Jessica. How's Daddy's little girl doing? I miss everything about you, especially your beautiful smile and laughter. I can still hear your voice in my dreams when you visit me. Thank you for those visits. They gave me reason to get up and out of bed all these years. (gathers his emotions)

Your baby boy Ced is all grown up. He has a family of his own, graduated with honors and is ready to change his world for the better. You know all this though. I've always believed that you were his guardian angel who kept him safe. You and your mom both....

We just went through a test. A test to see how much he wanted to reach his goals, and how much I wanted to keep my promise to you of taking care of him. I was so scared for him and I didn't want to disappoint you. I just couldn't......**(wipes his eyes)**

I hope you are proud of the both of us.

Look out for your mama until I see you both again. Visit me anytime. Bye Baby.

(he wraps up both urns carefully and puts them back into his bag. Rises from the bench and exits)

Canary Park

(From night to day, the lights depict time moving on. Fatimah and Ced arrive, laughing, playing, holding hands, happy and enjoying life.)

Ced

I want to thank you for all you've done for me Tima. I wasn't trying to push you away.

Fatimah

Yes, you were Ced. I understood though. You had a lot of pressure on you.

Ced

Life could change in a second. I went from being on top of the world to the bottom. **(snaps his fingers)** Just like that.

Fatimah

I wasn't going to let you go Ced. Not without a fight. I had to do something to save our family. You already know.

Ced

I love you for that... That snitch rule takes on a different feel when it's your family that's affected.

Fatimah

You better love me....all the time we've been together.

Yeah it's different when it's close to home. Our people don't trust the police. Who could blame us? At the same time, if we agree not to talk to police, then we have to do the policing in our community, whatever that looks like.

Ced

I leave for the Airforce next month. **(gesturing nervously)** I want to talk to you about something.

It's like ... .Let's get....

Cause after I finish boot camp....

Then I'll know exactly....

well I mean will you ah....?

Cause I'll be stationed in....and I need you and CJ with...So... yea......**(fanning himself)** It's hot.

Canary Park

Fatimah

You're sweating Baby. You okay? I thought my mama just had hot flashes.

Ced

Are you hot Tima?

Fatimah

No. I'm good.

Ced

Will you? **(coughs)**

Will you? **(sneezes)**

Fatimah

Ced are you asking me to marry you?

Ced

Well……a little bit **(wipes his brow and takes a deep breath and attempts to speak, but nothing comes out.)**

Fatimah

Yes… Ced…I will absolutely, definitely marry you.

Ced

Whew....**(Ced does a celebratory dance, they hug a deep relieved embrace, then Ced gets down on a knee and places a ring on her finger.)** This was my grandmother's ring. It's the only possession of her that I kept. I knew I would give it to you one day. Will you accept it?

Fatimah

Ced, this is so beautiful. Of course I'll accept it. It's an honor. **(she flaunts the ring and jumps up and down excitedly and improvises a little dance and song as Ced watches full of pride.)** Fatimah's getting married. She's marrying Ceddy. We have a family. Tima's ready!

Ced

While I'm in service I want you to go to school, get your law degree, then I'll go after. I'll take care of you and CJ.

Fatimah

I believe you, my love. I believe you. We'll take care of each other.

Canary Park

(RayRay enters, he approaches Fatimah and Ced and they are taken back by his change. His wears a shirt and tie and his energy has shifted. He smiles genuinely.)

RayRay

My people!

Ced and Fatimah

RayRay?!

RayRay

Yeah it's me.

Ced

Man we ain't seen you in weeks.

RayRay

I've been laying low. I'm through with running these streets.

Fatimah

It's good to hear that RayRay.

RayRay

Yea, Shay and me, we're having a baby girl. I realized I didn't have anything to give them, except for this life. I couldn't protect them as long as I was in these streets.

Ced

So what's next?

RayRay

Following your lead. I finally finished my GED and signed up for the Marines. I'm a learn everything about guns. Legally. For free. Heading out to Lancaster till it's time for bootcamp next winter. Our baby will be here by then. It's a fresh start, a chance to see the world and get out of LA.

Ced

That's great Bro.

RayRay

I never got a chance to tell you but, I appreciate you for not, you know.... mentioning my name. It must've been hard on you. You was always like a little brother to me, even though we took different paths.

Fatimah

Yea you appreciated him so much that you were willing to let him ruin his life. What type of friend does that?

Ced

Fatimah…..

RayRay

No she's right. I was blinded by money, and the power.

You both didn't deserve that. Had I been in the same position…..**(pausing; thinking)** To get locked up for something I didn't do for these goons around here. **(shaking his head no)** Probably would've just ate whatever time they gave me. Now, I wouldn't do it. I have too much to risk.

Ced

What made you realize that?

RayRay

YG. He was a psychopath. He had no rules. I realized I was surrounded by a bunch of YG's. I had to be more ruthless than them to keep everybody in line. I respect the game, but who wants to keep up that energy? It's only a matter of time before some other person wants to prove themselves.

Fatimah

YG was murdered a week before the trial began RayRay. What a coincidence.

RayRay

(thinking before responding, sits down on the bench)

These streets work in mysterious ways.

Murdered…Sacrificed…either way, with his death came freedom…for all of us.

Ced

So you had nothing to do with it?

RayRay

Canary Park

That's actually the question I have for you two, your grandfather and that crazy, what's his name?......Junebug.

Fatimah

You're deflecting RayRay. Answer the question.

RayRay

If I had to make a bet on who did it, I would first look at you as two suspects. He was about to destroy your family.**(There's an uncomfortable silence as they all look into each other's eyes.)**

So....At least we can agree that YG had a habit of making the wrong moves, with everyone he came into contact with. All the time.

Everyone had a motive. You, me, the twins, the connects he mentioned, and who knows what else he did to make people hate him?

Ced

Is that a confession?

RayRay

That's called deflecting Ced, and no, it's a statement not a confession.

Canary Park

Fatimah

You expect us to believe that?

RayRay

Believe what you want Fatimah. Can't count out the gatekeepers either.

Ced

What are gatekeepers? **(sits down critically thinking.)**

RayRay

They clean up our mess and protect the innocent. Protect instead of hurting my people. That's what I want to do. I want to be a gatekeeper.

Fatimah

Speaking on protecting the innocent.

RayRay. You owe me 3 thousand dollars. That's pocket change for you, but I need my hard earned "innocent" money back. Me and my man, I mean my fiance, got plans.

RayRay

Canary Park

How I owe you?

Fatimah

Where do you think YG got that money from that day?

RayRay

(pauses, thinking) Oh so, you.....I got it now.

Fatimah, you really had me fooled that day you. **(laughing)** Obviously, you really fooled him too.

Fatimah

And….where's my money RayRay?

RayRay

Say less. You got CashApp?

Fatimah

You know I do. **(hands him her phone)** Here's my account.

RayRay

(RayRay takes out his phone to complete the transaction.)

Done.

Canary Park

Fatimah

(checking her phone until the confirmation comes through.)

Looks kind of light RayRay. I deserve interest for all we've been through.

RayRay **(laughs until he sees that she is serious when she puts her hand on her hips while he makes another transfer.)**

Fatimah. Sister. You are not playing about your money. By the way, congrats on your engagement. Consider this an early wedding gift.

Fatimah

(looks at her phone) That'll do. Thank you.

RayRay

Tell your grandfather I said thank you.

Ced

For what?

RayRay

Canary Park

For opening my eyes and giving me options. There's a bigger world than Canary Park.

(RayRay hugs both Ced and Fatimah.)

Ced

RayRay...

RayRay

What's up Ced?

Ced

Who is Junebug?

RayRay

It's a long story. **(RayRay laughs as they exit)**

Canary Park

Act 2 Scene 5

(Enter Junebug with his shopping cart.

He takes out his radio and finds the perfect tune,

claps his hands and does a little two step.

He removes his broom and sweeps the stage and uses a dustpan to throw the trash away.

Next he takes out his rag and wipes down the benches.

Afterwards, Junebug takes a few flower pots from his cart and places them in various spots on stage.

He looks around and faces the audience. Smiles at them, then takes out his rag and wipes the air in front of him.

Satisfied, Junebug spreads his arms and closes them, embracing everyone then bows.

Canary Park

Finally, he grabs his shopping cart, waves at everyone and exits all while in rhythm with the beat.)

<u>Curtains Close.</u>

Canary Park

Peace.

Thank you for your support.

Essential questions revisited

4. If you witness a crime that brings harm to members of a family or community, will you stay silent or speak up?
5. How do we police our own community if we do not want the law involved with our affairs?
6. Whose responsibility is it to protect the innocent?

www.ingramcontent.com/pod-product-compliance
Lightning Source LLC
Chambersburg PA
CBHW071122090426
42736CB00012B/1982